GURDJIEFF — THE MAN AND HIS WORK

GURDJIEFF
The Man and his Work
An Introduction

Martin Ekker

Eureka Editions

Original Dutch Edition: 1968
Third printing: 1984

© EUREKA EDITIONS 2005

ISBN-10: 907239545X
ISBN-13: 9789072395450

Foreword

This little book has been written for those who are searching; for those who have a feeling, whether distinct or vague, that this life entrusted to us must have an infinitely deeper meaning than the pursuance of the aims their lives have been centred upon until now.

For those it will try to tell something about the life and work of one of the most remarkable men of this (the 20th) century.

I myself gladly testify how deep an impression the ideas of Gurdjieff on Man, on his relation to the great world process, and on the vision of the essential unity of everything existing, made on me at my very first acquaintance with them; and above all, to how in the course of time I have learned to experience these ideas and the practical philosophy of life based on them as *workable*. Workable in the sense that they can produce a real change in ourselves and effectively feed and guide us in our growth towards inner freedom and consciousness.

Only flashes perhaps in the beginning, but in these flashes of a fullness and intensity that are possible, we experience in all sharpness the poverty and deficiency of the level on which we usually live. This intensifies our longing and the realization of how much we need guidance and support in our search. That is why this work has grown into the central factor that gives my life a direction and meaning which I had not thought possible before and for which I am grateful in the depth of my being.

In what follows I leave the word as far as possible to Gurdjieff himself and to those who were closest to him. In this brief writing only a few indications can be given. It is my earnest wish that these may make many readers thirst for more.

M.H.E., Bosch en Duin, Holland, 1968

This booklet was written more than 50 years ago as an introduction to Gurdjieff's ideas.

As it was felt that it can still serve this purpose, this English edition has been prepared.

A few pages, describing the books of Gurdjieff and the Work at that time, were left out, because they were considered less relevant now than at that time.

Man a being with inconceivably great possibilities

According to Gurdjieff man, every man, has been endowed by nature with inconceivably great possibilities. By developing these he is able to become a Man in the true sense of the word. This is the sublime aim for which this life has been given to him.

These possibilities, however, are present in him as a germ, and can only be realized by intentional and meaningful 'work on oneself'.

The basis upon which this 'work on ourselves' is to be founded has been almost entirely lost; often we do not even suspect that such a thing exists or might exist. The factors of our conditioning - education and environment - do not point in this direction, with the result that man develops into a 'man' in quotation marks, as Gurdjieff puts it, a caricature as compared with what he could and should be.

Gurdjieff's youth and vocation

According to the Russian calendar George Ivanovitch Gurdjieff was born on January 1, 1877, in a region close to the Persian border which had been recently conquered by Russia in a war against the Turks. His mother was Armenian, his father of Ionian-Greek descent.

This Trans-Caucasian area is a melting pot of varied races and peoples: Russians, Greeks, Turkomans, Tartars, Armenians .... It was a land saturated with old traditions and customs, where often the miraculous, the hidden, was experienced as more real and meaningful than the visible every day world.

Growing up in these surroundings, and under the influence of his father and first tutors, the young Gurdjieff became convinced of three things: firstly, that life essentially has a meaning of quite another dimension than the one we succeed in realizing under the usual conditions; secondly, that in earlier times a knowledge existed of this meaning and of the way towards realizing it in oneself; and thirdly, that there must be certain communities in which this knowledge still exists, at least in part, and is being put into practice. And an overwhelming desire arose in him, a longing to fathom the secret of life.

Search and finding of sources of true knowledge

Gurdjieff surrenders himself completely to this longing. There follows a long period of adventurous and often dangerous expeditions through the Middle East, Africa and Central Asia, searching for the sources of this knowledge. Gurdjieff records these adventures in his book *Meetings with Remarkable Men*.

Around the beginning of the first world war we meet Gurdjieff again in Moscow. He is a different man now, a man who has not only found the knowledge which he was searching, but who has actually *become* this knowledge. And here begins the task he has set himself as the goal of his life: to transmit this knowledge and the way towards it in a form accessible in our days for the man who is rooted in Western culture, and so can guide him towards consciousness and inner freedom. He is working with small groups of pupils to whom he transmits the necessary knowledge and whom he stimulates by showing them an inexhaustible variety of forms of 'work on oneself'.

Ouspensky

It is in this period, in the spring of 1915, that P.D. Ouspensky comes into contact with Gurdjieff.

This Russian, born in 1876, was at that time already well-known as a thinker in the domains of philosophy and psychology, and above all as a pioneer in the field of scientific reconnaissance into the world hidden behind the world of the senses. He had published a book: *The Fourth Dimension* in 1909, and in 1912 *Tertium Organum*.

4

Ouspensky's desire to penetrate into the unknown had led him, a short time before the first world war, on a search through Egypt, Ceylon and India. His aim was to come into contact with 'schools'.

On his travels he arrived at the conviction that 'the East' did possess real knowledge, but was hiding it far better than he had expected.

His acquaintance with Gurdjieff

His coming into contact with Gurdjieff means a turning point in Ouspensky's life. He himself being a person of great inner strength and outstanding intelligence, feels at once that he is in the presence of a man of an altogether different dimension. This becomes already apparent at their first meeting. The atmosphere and environment into which Gurdjieff ushers him, give the very methodical Ouspensky an unreal feeling and he experiences an almost irresistable impulse to run away. At the same time his intuition tells him that Gurdjieff possesses that very knowledge for which he has been looking and longing so long. "I was most of all interested in the *connectedness* of everything he said. I already felt that his ideas were not detached one from the other ...., but made one whole, of which, as yet, I saw only some of the pieces." And later, when his intuition had grown into a deeper conviction, he writes: "Now, when I had begun to realize what a tremendous value these ideas had, I became almost terrified at the thought of how easily I could have passed them by, how easily I could have known nothing whatever of G.'s existence."

'In Search of the Miraculous'

These and the following quotations are from Ouspensky's book *In Search of the Miraculous; Fragments of an unknown Teaching*, a fascinating account of the seven year period of intensive work under the direction of Gurdjieff.

5

Ouspensky never published this account during his life; it was published after his death in 1947 with Gurdjieff's agreement, and appeared in 1950 both in French and English.

Its great value consists in the almost verbatim accounts of Ouspensky's discussions with Gurdjieff, and of the talks by the latter in group meetings (Ouspensky, who had a phenomenal memory, reconstructed these without notes). In this we possess the most reliable source in the available literature for the study of Gurdjieff's teaching.

The honesty with which Ouspensky relates his own questions and reactions and those of the other group members, as well as the unexpected turn given by Gurdjieff to each topic, make a book that grips us as an adventure story or novel. It is indeed the description of the greatest adventure conceivable: the recognition of a new reality in which our life acquires an unknown and deep meaning.

We experience with Ouspensky how the picture of the whole reveals itself to him with ever greater clarity, "like figures or a landscape which gradually appears in the developing of a photographic plate". In another place he writes: "In looking back now I cannot help being astonished at the speed with which G. transmitted to us the principal ideas of his system. Of course a great deal depended upon his manner of exposition, upon his astonishing capacity for bringing into prominence all principal and essential points and for not going into unnecessary details until the principal points had been understood."

Gurdjieff's teaching and official science

Ouspensky speaks about Gurdjieff's 'system' and on other occasions about his 'ideas'. However, these terms should be understood as indications only. It is definitely not a system in the sense of philosophical or other systems with which we are familiar, nor are they ideas in the sense of unconnected concepts or thought constructions. 'Fragments' is perhaps the best term: fragments of an integral knowledge, or, as in the subtitle of Ouspensky's book: fragments of an unknown teaching.

This knowledge has a basis, an approach and an aim quite different from our contemporary 'official' science; and because we have been indoctrinated in the latter through education and are interwoven with it through our environment, it is difficult for us to penetrate into this other knowledge.

Contemporary science investigates the phenomenal world surrounding us and strives above all to make phenomena predictable and wherever possible controllable. Thus its search is primarily oriented towards the periphery. Our knowledge of phenomena continuously increases and becomes more differentiated, and this unavoidably leads towards an ever growing specialization. In so far as science is interested in the central laws underlying phenomena, it tries to deduce these laws from its knowledge of the phenomenal world.

This science has undeniably yielded spectacular results in its own field. This attitude, however, resulted in the separation of religion and science which reached its culmination in the 19th century and which, but for a few shining exceptions, still rules contemporary thought. Instead of being led by reverence for God's creation, scientific investigation is for the far greater part oriented towards subjugating nature so as to make it satisfy our needs. "Only thought", says Gurdjieff, "as theoretical and as far removed from fact as modern European thought could have conceived the evolution of man to be possible *apart from surrounding nature*, or have regarded the evolution of man as a gradual *conquest of nature.*"

According to Gurdjieff it is first of all the knowledge about ourselves and our place and function in the great world process that is important to man. This he calls 'true' or 'real' knowledge, in the sense that it alone can teach us to understand what it means to 'make the most of our talents', and so help us in our striving for real fulfilment of the meaning of our life.

The fundamental unity of everything existing

"One of the most central of the ideas of objective knowledge", says Gurdjieff, "is the idea of the unity of everything, of unity in diversity."

That is why true knowledge will always aim at the fathoming of this unity, of the interconnectedness of all existing things. That is also why true knowledge, of whatever thing or phenomenon, is always connected with its meaning and function in the greater whole of which it forms a part. This knowledge can never be built up starting from an examination directed towards the parts, because the whole is of an essentially different order from the sum total of the component parts, and all endeavours to penetrate on the basis of our fragmentary knowledge of the latter into the meaning of the whole, are inevitably fruitless.

The connectedness of all existing things finds its expression in the fact that, as Gurdjieff says, laws are the same everywhere, in the world as well as in man. This was already postulated in the age-old saying of the Emerald Tablets of Hermes Trismegistus: "As above, so below". That is why Gurdjieff says: "In right knowledge the study of man must proceed on parallel lines with the study of the world, and the study of the world must run parallel with the study of man,"

Accordingly in Ouspensky's book we find unfolded, hand in hand with a psychology of man directed towards growth to inner freedom and consciousness, Gurdjieff's exposition of a cosmology of breath-taking majesty: a conception of the universe as consisting of worlds within worlds, mutually penetrating each other and with which we are connected in different ways. Also the fundamental laws are discussed, upon which the creation and the maintenance of these worlds are based.

Higher knowledge connected with higher consciousness

The result of this connectedness is that true knowledge can never be obtained by studying exclusively the perceptible world of the senses which surrounds us, us, a world of which we are, as it were, the accidental spectators. Linked up with the division to which we have referred, that so deeply penetrates our scientific thinking, is the striving to exclude to the highest possible extent every subjective factor from our observations, so as to gain 'objective' knowledge.

The higher knowledge about which Gurdjieff is speaking, is of an entirely different order. It is connected with an enlargement of our consciousness and cannot be known by methods of investigation and analysis which are rooted in our normal cognitive faculty. Ouspensky writes in his book: "One thing I understood even then with undoubted clarity, that no phenomena of a higher order, that is transcending the category of ordinary things observable every day .... can be observed or investigated by *ordinary means,* in an ordinary state of consciousness."

The transmission of true knowledge

This is also the reason why true knowledge cannot be transmitted in the ordinary sense of the word. Only the way towards it can be shown to us, so that we can, together with the enlargement of our consciousness, penetrate it.

9

"The acquisition or transmission of true knowledge", says Gurdjieff, "demands great labour and great effort both of him who receives and of him who gives. And those who possess this knowledge are doing everything they can to transmit it to the greatest possible number of people, to facilitate people's approach to it and enable them to prepare themselves to receive the truth."

Faith based on authority unnecessary and undesirable

We seldom realize the fact that almost all our personal knowledge has been borrowed from others. This kind of knowledge may be of use in the technical domain, but as soon as our own being and our relation to the great whole of the world surrounding us are involved, such cheaply obtained knowledge, not being rooted in true understanding, can only be barren; in the sense that it cannot provide a contribution to our growth towards consciousness and inner freedom.

Gurdjieff calls the way given by him the 'fourth way', as distinct from the 'traditional' ways of the 'fakir', the 'monk' and the 'yogi'. And he stresses the point that on this way we should not do anything without understanding why we are doing it. "No 'faith' is required on the fourth way", he says; "on the contrary, faith of any kind is opposed to the fourth way." And on another occasion: "What is required is simply a little trust and even that only for a little while, for the sooner a man begins to verify all he hears, the better it is for him."

Understanding necessary before anything else

Thus understanding is a first requirement on the fourth way. But this understanding goes far beyond a mere assimilation and processing by the mind. It implies experiencing the truth and the rightness of something with our whole being; only then can we really understand.

10

This understanding can only be obtained together with inner growth. "Understanding", says Gurdjieff, "depends upon the relation of knowledge to being. Understanding is the resultant of knowledge and being." The essential difference between knowing and understanding will become clear when we think of practical activities such as driving a car or typing; in these fields we are quite aware of the fact that there is a great difference between a mere knowing what we must do and wholly assimilating it with our being so as to be able to do it faultlessly.

That is the reason why, at the beginning, we can only be entrusted with fragments of the true knowledge about ourselves and the world. But when we work seriously with these purposely chosen fragments, they will transform themselves into living experience and gradually develop within us the possibility to understand more and more.

Evolution

The evolution in which man should be interested before anything else, is his own inner evolution. "The evolution of man", says Gurdjieff, "can be taken as the development in him of those powers and possibilities which never develop by themselves, that is mechanically." And on another occasion: "In speaking of evolution it is necessary to understand from the outset that no mechanical evolution is possible. The evolution of man is the evolution of his consciousness. *And 'consciousness' cannot evolve unconsciously.* The evolution of man is the evolution of his will, and 'will' cannot evolve involuntarily. The evolution of man is the evolution of his power of doing, and 'doing' cannot be the result of things which 'happen'."

Essence and personality

In speaking about the structure of man's being Gurdjieff introduces the distinction between 'essence' and 'personality'. "It must be understood", he says, "that man consists of two parts: *essence* and *personality*. Essence in man is what is *his own*. Personality in man is what is 'not his own'. 'Not his own' means what has come from outside, what he has learned, or reflects, all traces of exterior impressions left in the memory and in the sensations, all words and movements that have been learned, all feelings created by imitation – all this is 'not his own', all this is personality .... In proportion as personality grows, essence manifests itself more and more rarely and more and more feebly, and it often happens that essence stops in its growth at a very early age and grows no further .... This means that everything we see (in such a person) is in reality 'not his own'.... The element that is 'not his own' differs from what is man's 'own' by the fact that it can be lost, altered, or taken away by artificial means" (Ouspensky describes in his book a very interesting demonstration by Gurdjieff of a temporary dispersal of personality) .... "It can be said that a man's individuality is his essence, grown up, mature .... If we take an average cultured man, we shall see that in the vast majority of cases his personality is the active element in him while his essence is the passive element. The inner growth of a man cannot begin so long as this order of things remains unchanged. Personality must become passive and essence must become active."

'Work on oneself'   True knowledge and inner evolution or inner growth are linked inseparably.

In the same way as we cannot obtain true knowledge for nothing, so our inner growth cannot proceed by itself. On the contrary, this highest good obtainable for man also requires the highest price: 'work on ourself', with a commitment of our whole being.

We will, however, never pay this price, never be able to pay this price, as long as we do not realize our present situation and the rich possibilities we pass by unused when we continue allowing ourselves to live as we live. And should a suspicion dawn in us that there is 'something wrong', then we simply cannot believe that it might be possible to bring about a real change.

The disease called 'tomorrow' We postpone until 'later on', when we 'will have time for it', when 'circumstances will be more favourable'. At present we are so much taken up by the demands of every day life and our professional and family responsibilities that we cannot, in good conscience, be asked *now* to spend time and energy on 'that kind of thing'.

In this work this attitude is called the disease of 'tomorrow'. However, 'tomorrow' remains 'tomorrow', day after day and year after year. Until perhaps in the evening of our life we realize the seriousness of our situation and the urgency to fulfil what is within our power to bring about a change.

But then it is too late. Because there is a time for everything, and the opportunity we leave unused *now*, will not come back 'later'. And according to Gurdjieff it is perhaps the greatest tragedy of human life that so many, as they begin to understand that something altogether different is required to give meaning to our lives, feel at the same time their incapacity to realize it. They have been spending the energy entrusted to them for 'work on themselves' on all kinds of trivialities of a transitory and doubtful nature.

On the 'fourth way' our field of work and learning is in ordinary life That is why the work says that the best, indeed the only time for 'work on oneself' is *now* and not 'tomorrow'. For this 'work on oneself' it is not necessary to turn away from the responsibilities of everyday life; on the contrary, on the fourth way we find our field of 'work' and learning exactly in the fullness

13

of every day life. This is in distinction from the three 'traditional' ways of the 'fakir', the 'monk' and the 'yogi', which do require a withdrawal from ordinary life. At the same time, according to Gurdjieff, this 'fourth way' is much quicker, because here the 'work on ourselves' simultaneously touches upon all sides of our being.

Moreover he says that there is a firm law according to which the circumstances in which we find ourselves at the present moment, are the best possible ones for starting this work; they are the reflection of how we are, and for that reason they form the ideal basis to study our 'being' in all its aspects and to begin to know it.

Our present situation   Gurdjieff uses several images to make us realize the situation in which we are. "We are living", he says, "in a house that is our legitimate heritage. But of this house we only know and inhabit the smallest and poorest room and do not even suspect that there are three more rooms, each of which is incomparably richer in accomodation and view than the preceding one."

On another occasion he says that we are living in a prison. We do not realize this and still less suspect that outside the prison there are people living free, whose highest aim it is to do all that is possible to help us escape.

Also he compares our situation to slavery. "One thing is certain", he says, "that man's slavery grows and increases. Man is becoming a willing slave. He no longer needs chains. He begins to grow fond of his slavery, to be proud of it. And this is the most terrible thing that can happen to a man."

Everything 'happens'   One of the basic ideas to which Gurdjieff comes back again and again relates to the mechanicalness of our manifestations. It is an

14

illusion that we, as we are, are able to do. Real doing requires an altogether different level of being than the one at which we ordinarily live. With us the situation is that, as we are, our thinking, feeling and acting are almost entirely determined by external influences, that 'it' thinks and 'it' feels and everything 'happens' with us, in exactly the same way as 'it' rains or 'it' freezes.

'Sleep' and awakening

According to Gurdjieff we go through life sleep-walking. "It may surprise you", he says, "if I say that the chief feature of a modern man's being which *explains everything else that is lacking in him* is *sleep*. A modern man lives in sleep, in sleep he is born and in sleep he dies .... What is called 'clear consciousness' is sleep, and a far more dangerous sleep than sleep at night in bed .... All that men say, all that they do, they say and do in sleep. All this can have no value whatever. Only awakening and what leads to awakening has a value in reality ....

How can one awaken? How can one escape this sleep? These questions are the most important, the most vital that can ever confront a man. But before this it is necessary to be convinced of the very fact of sleep."

"There is nothing new in the idea of sleep. People have been told almost since the creation of the world that they are asleep and that they must awaken. How many times is this said in the Gospels, for instance? 'Awake', 'watch', 'sleep not'. Christ's disciples even slept when he was praying in the Garden of Gethsemane for the last time .... I tell you seriously that I have been asked several times why nothing is said about sleep in the Gospels. Although it is there spoken of almost on every page. This simply shows that people read the Gospels in sleep."

On another occasion he is speaking about the nature of our sleep and the forces that prevent us from awakening: "There are a thousand things which prevent a man from awakening,

15

which keep him in the power of his dreams. In order to act consciously with the intention of awakening, it is necessary to know the nature of the forces which keep man in a state of sleep."

"First of all it must be realized that the sleep in which man exists is not normal but hypnotic sleep. Man is hypnotized and this hypnotic state is continuously maintained and strengthened in him. One would think that there are forces for whom it is useful and profitable to keep man in a hypnotic state and prevent him from seeing the truth and understanding his position."

The tale of the magician and the sheep Gurdjieff illustrates this with the tale of the magician and the sheep: "There is an Eastern tale which speaks about a very rich magician who had a great many sheep. But at the same time this magician was very mean. He did not want to hire shepherds, nor did he want to erect a fence about the pasture where his sheep were grazing. The sheep consequently often wandered into the forest, fell into ravines, and so on, and above all they ran away, for they knew that the magician wanted their flesh and skins and this they did not like.

"At last the magician found a remedy. He *hypnotized* his sheep and suggested to them first of all that they were immortal and that no harm was being done to them when they were skinned, that, on the contrary, it would be very good for them and even pleasant; secondly he suggested that the magician was a *good master* who loved his flock so much that he was ready to do anything in the world for them; and in the third place he suggested to them that if anything at all were going to happen to them it was not going to happen just then, at any rate not that day, and *therefore* they had no need to think about it. Further the magician suggested to his sheep that they were not sheep at all; to some of them he suggested that they

16

were *lions*, to others that they were *eagles*, to others that they were *men*, and to others that they were *magicians*."

"And after this all his cares and worries about the sheep came to an end. They never ran away again but quietly awaited the time when the magician would require their flesh and skins."

'Buffers' How do we manage to live with all our inner confusion and contradictions? According to Gurdjieff this is made possible by a special type of artificial appliance which has developed in our functional apparatus and which he calls 'buffers'. "'Buffer'",he says, "is a term which requires special explanation. We know what 'buffers' on railway carriages are. They are the contrivances which lessen the shock when carriages or trucks strike one another …. Exactly the same appliances are to be found within man. They are created, not by nature but by man himself, although involuntarily. The cause of their appearance is the existence in man of many contradictions; contradictions of opinions, feelings, sympathies, words, and actions …. If a man were to feel all these contradictions, he would feel what he really is. He would feel that he is mad …. He must either destroy contradictions or cease to see and to feel them. A man cannot destroy contradictions" (that is, not without conscious and intentional 'work on oneself'). "But if 'buffers' are created in him he can cease to feel them and he will not feel the impact from the clash of contradictory views, contradictory emotions, contradictory words." "Conscience is possible only in the absence of 'buffers'."

Effort without tension 'Work on oneself' to awake from this hypnotic sleep requires a great effort. This effort, however, is of an entirely different nature from the efforts we are used to in ordinary life when we set our teeth into something in order to reach a desired goal or to force ourselves to comply with what we consider to be our duty.

Rather it is the exact opposite, an effort without tension, which is directed towards liberating ourselves from the quite useless tensions in which we are constantly caught. It is a state of preparedness, an intensity and sensitivity without forcing, an opening up of ourselves and providing room for that which is real inside and outside of us.

The very subtlety of it, however, makes this effort so difficult, for it requires great inner alertness. That is the reason why, next to the earnestness of our commitment, the quality of our efforts is so important for our progress. This especially applies to the two closely related things around which, at the beginning and during a long time to come, the 'work on oneself' revolves: self-remembering and self-knowledge.

Self-remembering   Self-remembering is the realizing of one's own being, as opposed to our being always and completely lost in whatever we are doing, thinking or feeling at a given moment, which, in the special language of this work is called being 'identified'. Self-remembering is experiencing that *I* am observing, *I* am noticing, *I* am thinking or feeling or doing, *I* am speaking or listening.

Once we begin to know the taste of self-remembering, we experience it as an entirely new dimension in our life: an inner certainty and freedom. We find a connectedness with the world outside us as well as with ourselves hitherto unknown.

"All that G. said", writes Ouspensky, "all that I myself thought, and especially all that my attempts at self-remembering had shown me, very soon convinced me that I was faced with an *entirely new problem which science and philosophy had not, so far, come across.*"

Without self-remembering we 'are' not: according to Gurdjieff we then only exist.

18

And at the same time we are aware of the fact that the pull of identification is inconceivably strong and that we can, as we are, remember ourselves only by flashes. However intense our longing may be, we immediately are identified, lost again.

In his book Ouspensky gives us a lively account of one of his first endeavours to remember himself and of his success and failure.

Self-knowledge and self-observation

"Without self-knowledge", says Gurdjieff, "without understanding the working and functions of his machine, man cannot be free, he cannot govern himself and he will always remain a slave, and a plaything of the forces acting upon him. This is why in all ancient teachings the first demand at the beginning of the way to liberation was: *'Know thyself'*."

And furthermore: "The chief method of self-study is self-observation. Without properly applied self-observation a man will never understand the connection and the correlation between the various functions of his machine, will never understand how and why on each separate occasion everything in him 'happens'."

Through self-observation we learn to know the meaning and structure of the miraculous apparatus with which we have been endowed and the undreamt of capacities of this apparatus when rightly used. We learn to distinguish the functions of this apparatus. They are, in their most simple sub-division: the thinking function, the feeling function and the instinctive-moving function, each one governed by its own centre, having its own memory and field of action. We also, however, learn to discern the peculiarities and obstinacies of this apparatus, to which we have been entirely blind so far. We experience how, as a result of this, we are its slave instead of the master; how this apparatus simply goes its own way and how true it is that everything 'happens' with us; and how, to quote the words of

St. Paul, "the good that I would I do not, but the evil which I would not, that I do".

The difficulties of right self-observation

Right self-observation is far more difficult than we suspect. Almost all of us have a picture of ourselves that is poles apart from reality. We unconditionally believe in this picture, causing it to exercise such hypnotic power over us that we simply ignore everything that is in contradiction to it. When once in a while we happen to be so confronted with the obvious truth about ourselves that we cannot escape it, we begin to justify ourselves. Or we fall into the opposite extreme of self-vilifying; or into analyzing.

These and similar automatic reactions immediately distract our attention, our self-observation is cut short abruptly and prematurely, thus not leading to a real experience about ourselves, which, by its intensity and inescapability could have been active and liberating.

Also there is a constant danger of working for 'results'. Results will come, but they are always different from what we foresee and can foresee. That is why, by striving for pre-conceived results and focusing our attention on them, we inevitably pass by the real results when they present themselves.

The urge to bring about a 'change'

Finally, there is the equally automatic impulse to bring about a change with respect to that which does not please us in ourselves. We are so firmly convinced that we can 'do'. So why should we not quickly and radically change such an unbecoming peculiarity?

This 'fighting against' is, with a few exceptions, not the way either. First of all – and this we know already from ordinary psychology – by combatting something, we generally only

20

reinforce it. This does not mean that, by going all out, we would not be able to suppress an undesired habit or quality. But then, according to Gurdjieff, a much more serious danger arises. "Everything in the machine is inter-connected", he says, "and every function is inevitably counterbalanced by some other function or by a whole series of other functions …. The machine is balanced in all its details at every moment of its activity. If a man observes in himself something that he dislikes and begins making efforts to alter it, he may succeed in obtaining a certain result. But together with this result he will inevitably obtain another result, which he does not in the least expect or desire and which he could not have suspected …. The machine strives to re-establish the balance and re-establishes it by creating a new function which the man could not have foreseen." And Gurdjieff proceeds to tell, for instance, how a man, in combatting his forgetfulness and absent-mindedness can grow irritable, pedantic, fault-finding and disagreeable, or stingy, jealous or something else.

Right self-observation leads to change

Real change, in the sense of awakening to a new consciousness, is the great goal of this work, but the shortest and especially the safest way to this goal is the seeming detour via self-observation.

The remarkable thing, moreover, is that this self-observation in itself already produces a change in us. "In observing himself", says Gurdjieff, "a man notices that self-observation itself brings about certain changes in his inner processes. He begins to understand that self-observation is an instrument of self-change, a means of awakening. By observing himself he throws, as it were, a ray of light onto his inner processes which have hitherto worked in complete darkness. And under the influence of this light the processes themselves begin to change. There are a great many chemical processes that can take place only in the absence of light. Exactly in the same way many psychic processes can take place only in the dark."

That is why getting to know ourselves, though admittedly extremely painful and disillusioning, is at the same time such a wonderful and liberating experience. And it is necessary, since inner growth is utterly impossible while we continue to live on a basis of illusion.

Right self-observation an art we have to learn
It follows that rightly conducted self-observation, observing without allowing ourselves to be distracted by our emotions, without self-justification on the one side or self-vilification on the other, without slipping away into analysis, without working for 'results' or wishing to combat and change immediately, yet with an intense interest and feeling of connectedness as well as an urge to penetrate the truth about ourselves, is an art that we really have to learn. It requires a control over our attention which can only be obtained by a great inner alertness and by self-remembering.

"Try to *remember yourselves* when you observe yourselves", Gurdjieff says in his group, "and later on tell me the results. Only those results will have any value that are accomplished by self-remembering. Otherwise you yourselves do not exist in your observations. In which case what are all your observations worth?"

Absence of unity in man
With self-observation we can experience with appalling clarity how all kinds of wonderful qualities and powers we ascribed to ourselves: consciousness, a permanent and unchangeable I, will, and the power to do, are entirely illusory. How, on the contrary, we consist of

22

many separate, mostly inane, small 'I''s, mutually exclusive and incompatible or not knowing one another at all, and which by turns take possession of us; how what we call '*will*' is merely the tyranny of accidental desires; how this causes everything to 'happen' with us and how we cannot in the true sense be responsible for our manifestations. "A *man*", says Gurdjieff, "is responsible, a *machine* is not responsible."

The treacherous thing is that all these persons living in us call themselves 'I'. "They consider themselves masters", says Gurdjieff, "and none wants to recognize another .... Imagine a country where everyone can be king for five minutes and do during these five minutes just what he likes with the whole kingdom. That is our life." And on another occasion: "A small accidental I may promise something, not to itself but to someone else at a certain moment, simply out of vanity or for amusement. Then it disappears, but the man, that is the whole combination of other I's who are quite innocent of this, may have to pay for it all his life. It is the tragedy of human being that any small I has the right to sign checks and promissory notes and the man, that is the Whole, has to meet them. People's whole lives often consist in paying off the promissory notes of small accidental I's."

Carriage, horse and driver   All the earlier mentioned faculties, as well as incomparably greater and richer ones, are potentially in us. They must be developed by intentional 'work on ourselves'. However, we will never seriously commit ourselves to this 'work on ourselves', nor will we be able to do so, as long as we are entangled in the illusion that we do possess these faculties already. Why should we exert ourselves to obtain something which we are convinced we already possess?

That is why Gurdjieff goes out of his way to give us, by means of appropriate images, a clear insight into our situation.

We will briefly relate one more, the Eastern allegory in which man is compared to a horse-driven carriage.

The driver on the box is the mind; the horse that pulls the carriage is our feelings and desires; the carriage itself is our body. The carriage is connected with the horse by the shaft, the horse with the driver by the reins.

There is, however, something utterly wrong. The driver, who should be watchful and feel responsible for the whole, sits on his box for the far greater part of the time befogged and day-dreaming; or he is gossiping with his comrades in a tavern and leaves horse and carriage unattended outside.

The horse never gets the care and food it needs, nor has it ever been trained for its task. Neglected as it is, it knows, in fact, only two impulses: food and sex.

The carriage itself is also badly neglected and has been patched up in several places. Originally, it was robustly built and designed for running on all kinds of roads. But since it is only used on the paved roads in town and never has to endure shocks, it is no longer shock-proof. As a consequence something breaks down at the first serious one.

Most serious, and indeed the cause of all evils, is the fact that there is no master who rules the whole and uses it with meaning and purpose, and whom the driver obeys. That is why the whole organisation has been degraded to the level of a hackney-carriage: every accidental passer-by can hire it and be driven somewhere without feeling any responsibility as to where he leaves it or in what condition.

**'Identification',
negative emotions
and 'considering'**

Through self-observation we also learn to recognize clearly the power of some aspects of our psyche that are more than anything else responsible for keeping us asleep.

'Identification' has already been mentioned. "'Identification'", says Gurdjieff, "is so common a quality that for purposes of observation it is difficult to separate it from everything else. Man is always in a state of identification, only the object of identification changes .... 'Identifying' is one of our most terrible foes, because it penetrates everywhere and deceives a man at the moment when it seems to him that he is struggling with it."

Further, we learn to know the important role negative emotions play in our lives: anger, irritation, anguish, suspicion, hate, the feeling of being wronged, jealousy, depression .... , an almost endless catalogue. We are used to accepting these as an unavoidable part of life, we justify them, even glorify them in art. They serve, however, no positive aim whatsoever and are only detrimental, by the power they exercise over us. Furthermore, through negative emotions there drains away from us that very energy so badly needed for 'work on ourselves'. To come to real growth, it is therefore unconditionally necessary to liberate ourselves from them; and it is possible to do so, because – and this is most important – the negative emotions are not ingrained in our being.

In addition there is, in the special language of this work, 'considering', or, more correctly: 'internal considering', which is 'identifying' with people. "On the most prevalent occasions", says Gurdjieff, "a man is identified with what others think about him, how they treat him, what attitude they show towards him." And also: "There is still another form of considering which can take a great deal of energy from a man. This form starts with a man beginning to think that he is *not considering another person enough*, that this other person is offended with him for not considering him sufficiently." In 'internal considering' everything revolves around our own tiny self; that is why it poisons all our relations with others and why we never can be really free and unimpeded in these relations, however much we may be craving for a deeper contact. "The opposite of internal considering", says Gurdjieff again, "and what is in part a means of fighting against it, is external considering. External considering is based upon an entirely different relationship towards people than internal

25

considering. It is adaptation towards people, to their understanding, to their requirements."

'Sacrifices' In the work we must be prepared to make sacrifices. "Without sacrifices", says Gurdjieff, "nothing can be obtained." But here again he throws an unexpected light on the matter. "If there is anything in the world", he says, "that people do not understand, it is the idea of sacrifice. They think they have to sacrifice something that they have. For example, I once said that they must sacrifice 'faith', 'tranquillity', 'health'. They understood this literally. As if they had either faith, tranquillity or health! All these words must be taken in quotation marks. *In actual fact they have to sacrifice only what they imagine they have but which in reality they do not have.* They must sacrifice their fantasies. But this is difficult for them, very difficult. It is much easier to sacrifice real things."

To begin at the beginning The decision to begin with work is an important step. "Because there is nothing worse", says Gurdjieff, "than to begin work on oneself and then leave it and find oneself between two stools; it is much better not to begin."

Also he stresses very seriously the point that we must begin at the beginning. In our greed and over-estimation of ourselves we too easily consider this as beneath our dignity and we tend to be far too ambitious. In this connection he says: "And principally (a man) must know how far he is willing to go, what he is willing to sacrifice. There is nothing more easy to say than *everything*. A man can never sacrifice everything and this can never be required of him."

The Armenian fairy-tale of the wolf and the sheep

Gurdjieff once more elucidates this with one of his striking illustrations, this time the Armenian fairy-tale of the wolf and the sheep: "Once there lived a wolf who slaughtered a great many sheep and reduced many people to tears. At length, I do not know why, he suddenly felt qualms of conscience and began to repent his life. So he decided to reform and to slaughter no more sheep. In order to do this seriously he went to a priest and asked him to hold a thanks-giving service. The priest began the service and the wolf stood weeping and praying in the church. The service was long. The wolf had slaughtered many of the priest's sheep, therefore the priest prayed earnestly that the wolf would indeed reform. Suddenly the wolf looked through a window and saw that the sheep were being driven home. He began to fidget, but the priest went on and on without end. At last the wolf could contain himself no longer and he shouted: "Finish it, priest! Or all the sheep will be driven home and I shall be left without supper!""

And Gurdjieff adds: "This is a very good fairy-tale, because it describes man very well. He is ready to sacrifice everything, but after all today's dinner is a different matter."

To become a Christian

The same urge to be realistic about our aspirations and aims is conveyed by Gurdjieff in his answers to such questions as: "How to be a real Christian?" and "How to stop wars?"

"First of all", he says, "it is necessary to understand that a Christian is not a man who calls himself a Christian or whom others call a Christian. A Christian is one who lives in accordance with Christ's precepts. Such as we are we cannot be Christians. In order to be Christians we must be able 'to do'. We cannot do; with us everything 'happens'. Christ says: "Love your enemies", but how can we love our enemies when we cannot even love our friends? Sometimes 'it loves' and sometimes 'it does not love'. Such as we are we cannot even really desire to be Christians, because, again, sometimes 'it desires' and sometimes 'it does not desire' .... To be a Christian means to be responsible. Responsibility comes later when a man even partially ceases to be a machine, and begins in fact, and not only in words, to desire to be a Christian."

Can wars be stopped?

"War", says Gurdjieff again, "is the result of the slavery in which man lives. Strictly speaking men are not to blame for war. War is due to cosmic forces, to planetary influences. But in men there is no resistance whatever against these influences, and there cannot be any, because men are slaves. If they were *men* and were capable of 'doing', they would be able to resist these influences and refrain from killing one another .... Wars are not decreasing, they are increasing, and war cannot be stopped by ordinary means. All these theories about universal peace, about peace conferences, and so on, are again simply laziness and hypocrisy. Men do not want to think about themselves, do not want to work on themselves, but think of how to make other people do what *they* want." And on another occasion: "How many times have I been asked here whether wars can be stopped? Certainly they can. For this it is only necessary that people should awaken. It seems a small thing. It is, however, the most difficult thing there can be, because this sleep is induced and maintained by the whole of surrounding life, by all surrounding conditions."

Other material in Ouspensky's book

These are some selected themes from the rich material in Ouspensky's book, ideas that refer mainly to the way in which Gurdjieff tries to make us realize our present situation and in which he gives us a general basis for 'work on oneself'. It is not possible, in the brief scope of this booklet, to give further indications about 'work on oneself' without giving a distorted picture.

Reluctantly, we must also limit ourselves to no more than mentioning Gurdjieff's stressing the necessity for common work in groups, his elaborations on the foundations of this group-work, the development of the groups themselves, the interesting experiments that Gurdjieff conducts, and the tasks he gives to his pupils.

The cosmological ideas must again remain untouched upon. To them a substantial part of the book is devoted, and they constitute an integral part of the whole because they are, in a sense, the compliment of the psychological ideas and give us an insight into the great world process and our meaningful place and responsibility in this process.

Our energy household

Before leaving Ouspensky's book, however, we will briefly mention one other important subject: our energy household. "The human organism", says Gurdjieff "represents a chemical factory planned for the possibility of a very large output. But in the ordinary conditions of life the output of this factory never reaches the full production possible to it, because only a small part of the machinery is used, which produces only that quantity of material necessary to maintain its own existence. Factory work of this kind is obviously uneconomic in the highest degree. The factory actually produces nothing – all its machinery, all its elaborate equipment, actually serve no purpose at all, in that it maintains only with difficulty its own existence."

The raw materials with which the factory of our organism works, are the food we eat and drink, the air we breathe, the impressions we receive. With the help of an interesting diagram Gurdjieff indicated how these three kinds of raw materials are refined in our organism and transformed into the finer matters or more potent energies that are required for the functioning of our different centres.

However, there is something wrong. On the one hand, the production of the higher energies remains much below what it should be, and on the other the far greater part of our energy is quite uselessly poured away.

We referred earlier to negative emotions as a drain on our energy. "Energy", Gurdjieff says, "is spent chiefly on unnecessary and unpleasant emotions, on the expectation of unpleasant things, possible and impossible, on bad moods, on unnecessary haste, nervousness, irritability, day-dreaming, and so on. Energy is wasted on the wrong work of centres; on unnecessary tensions of the muscles out of all proportion to the work produced; on perpetual chatter which absorbs an enormous amount of energy; on the 'interest' continually taken in things happening around us or to other people and having in fact no interest whatever; on the constant waste of the force of 'attention'; and so on, and so on."

And as regards the production of the higher energies on which our inner growth and the development of higher faculties depend, Gurdjieff shows us, with the help of the above-mentioned diagram, at which point exactly this production stagnates and must continue to stagnate, when we let ourselves live as we are living, and where the point of application is to be located in order to increase this production.

Gurdjieff's books   The writings Gurdjieff left us are unique in every respect. They comprise three series. The publication of the first series was prepared by Gurdjieff himself a short time before his death. It was published in English in 1950 under the title *All and Everything*, shortly afterwards in German and in 1957 in French under the title *Récits de Belzébuth à son petit-fils – critique objectivement impartial de la vie des hommes* (*Beelzebub's Tales to His Grandson – an Objectively Impartial Criticism of the Life of Man*). The second series, called *Meetings with Remarkable Men* was published in 1960 in French and in 1963 in English. The title of the third series is *Life is Real Only Then, When 'I Am'*.

At the beginning of the first series we find a description of the aims Gurdjieff has put himself with these writings:

"All written according to entirely new principles of logical reasoning and strictly directed towards the solution of the following three cardinal problems:

> FIRST SERIES: To destroy, mercilessly, without any compromises whatsoever, in the mentation and feelings of the reader, the beliefs and views, by centuries rooted in him, about everything existing in the world.

> SECOND SERIES: To acquaint the reader with the material required for a new creation and to prove the soundness and good quality of it.

> THIRD SERIES: To assist the arising, in the mentation and in the feelings of the reader, of a veritable, non-fantastic representation, not of that illusory world which he now perceives, but of the world existing in reality."

But the greatest adventure about which Gurdjieff is writing is always his inner adventure. And he who reads his books with true interest and attention will hear over and over again the deep echo of the fundamental teaching of the author: that the life of man has a real meaning only when it is borne by the striving for consciousness and for being anchored in his conscience.

Afterword

Coming to the end of this little book we will try to face the question of Gurdjieff's significance in our present time and for us personally.

We have seen that Gurdjieff brought to the West a knowledge almost entirely lost. This knowledge is embodied in various forms: in books, in the movements and films, in music. It embraces ideas of exceptional force and depth, and of a great dynamism, as is proved by the fact that they penetrate contemporary thinking more and more, even though the source is often not acknowledged.

But there is also something of an altogether different dimension: Gurdjieff appeals to us, he calls us to awaken, to awaken to an entirely new reality. He calls, because he suffers from the inner chaos in which man lives, and because of which he is the will-less victim of the ever increasing power of violence and of threats of inconceivable magnitude. Gurdjieff is the knowledge he teaches, he lives the new reality of which he speaks. That is why his call is so penetrating and so personal.

Gurdjieff challenges us. We do not know who we are and do not know the forces governing our existence. Even worse is that we evade these and similar questions, turn away from them. Gurdjieff forces us to face them, independently, as mature men, and not to flee away into the supposed security of our familiar concepts. He is pointed and merciless in undermining our belief in these; and in cutting away all that is not genuine in us.

But in supporting an earnest striving for self-realization and true 'being' he is of an infinite generosity and puts to use in full the amazing many-sidedness of his rich personality.

That is why the work started by Gurdjieff is so strong and so undiminishingly alive. The soil has proved to be well-prepared. Also the seed sown by him has proved to be sound. This soundness finds expression in the deepening enrichment

33

the work is undergoing under the direction of Gurdjieff's closest pupils. There is no formal organisation; yet the inner consistency is all the greater for this. The main centres are in Paris, New York, London, Caracas; and many groups have been formed in different towns in the United States, France, England, Canada, Switzerland, Holland, Germany, Mexico and other Latin-American countries.

Selected bibliography

Gurdjieff, G.I., *All and Everything*, An Objectively Impartial Criticism of the Life of Man or Beelzebub's Tales to His Grandson, Harcourt, Brace & Co, New York 1950.

Gurdjieff, G.I., *Meetings with Remarkable Men*, Routledge & Kegan Paul, London, 1963.

Gurdjieff, G.I., *Life is Real Only Then, When 'I Am,'* Triangle Editions, New York, 1978.

Gurdjieff, G.I., *Views from the Real World*. Early Talks in Moscow, Essentuki, Tiflis, Berlin, London, Paris, New York and Chicago As Recollected By His Pupils. Routledge & Co, London, 1973.

Ouspensky, P.D., *In Search of the Miraculous*, Harcourt, Brace & World, New York, 1949.

An extensive bibiography is compiled by Walter Driscoll and freely available from http://www.gurdjieff-bibliography.com

EUREKA EDITIONS
Herenstraat 4 A
3512 kc Utrecht
The Netherlands

E-BOOK AND PRINT-ON-DEMAND

MAY 2020

info@eurekaeditions.com
www.eurekaeditions.com

CPSIA information can be obtained
at www.ICGtesting.com
Printed in the USA
BVHW030724070323
659806BV00024B/196